Table of Content

INTRODUCTION

You are reading a book about parenting and dealing with children. You probably have children/foster children of your own or you are professionally involved with children, parents or caregivers.

Parenting challenges are part of everyday life. Every mother and father reaches their own limits at times or experiences times where a disastrous situation seems to repeat itself for the hundredth time. In theory, you know the right things to do. However, you may seem simply unable to put your knowledge into practice and act accordingly. The result: arguments, conflicts, screaming, tears.

During my 19 years of therapeutic and educational work with children, adolescents and parents, I noticed that a few key problems seem to appear over and over again.

And these are exactly the subject of this book. No scientific theories, no lengthy explanations – the focus is on you and your desire to get a grip on recurrent conflicts. Written in clear and straightforward language, I want to propose hands-on solutions to sixteen everyday challenges when raising children. I hope in the end you will understand not only your child better, but yourself in dealing with your child.

I am a practical person. Of course, it would be possible to set out all the procedures described theoretically and to provide scientific explanations. But then this book would have been an overly theoretical book with 300 pages. Would you like to read a non-fiction book of 300 pages? Do you have the time?

In addition, I am convinced that you need no theoretical model to solve the conflicts described here. You need hands-on solutions that you can implement in everyday life.

You need a view from the outside, a change of perspective, in order to understand why sometimes it is so damn hard to put into effect your own ideas of good parenting.

Maybe you or teachers in your community think raising children depends on many additional variables not mentioned in this book. You are right! It takes a village to raise a child; early childhood education and school; the social environment, all this needs to be considered, as well as parents and siblings. But this book is primarily about what y o u can do, to solve certain recurrent problems.

It is inevitable that you will not be able to relate completely to each example and that you could describe your situation more specifically and comprehensively. Yet, people often differ from each other less than we think. There are typical situations that anyone who has worked with children, knows and recognizes, where we are at our wit's end and ask ourselves, why is everything so hard?

The recommendations of this book are independent of your child's age. Of course, it would be great if you could start implementing them in the first year of your child's life. If this has not been possible, you can start at any time regardless of the age of the children you live with or meet.

This book is neither a magic potion nor does it replace counseling. It is meant as a useful guide. At the end of each chapter you will find an "Ideas Toolkit". The Ideas Toolkit does not start initially with the "difficult" child, instead it begins with you; the way you think and feel, your experience. Why is it so hard to get your child to do what you want? What prevents you from achieving your child-raising ideals?

The Ideas Toolkit shows you, in a nutshell, possible causes and supports you to re-assess and ameliorate a situation. While this guide to self-help is consciously written in easy language using concrete terms, it carries the seed for deeply rooted change. And this change starts with you. Right now. I hope you will enjoy reading the book, which hopefully will help you enjoy the company of your child/children.

Yours,

Heiko Pust

1. PRAISE FOR EVERY LITTLE THING?

When you child starts to take action, when he[1] tries something new, is brave or has learned something new, please praise him.

Praise your child with loving words and an eagerness that might sound almost exaggerated to the ears of an adult. Repeat it even if the child does something very similar to before. If you accompany your praise with a caress, a hug or loving pat, the praise will be received even better. Boosted by a greater self-confidence, your child will tackle the next challenge.

If your child, for example, comes to you with a picture he has drawn (maybe the first one he has ever drawn) then it should be completely unimportant how he has painted or drawn the picture. At that moment it is the best and most beautiful picture you have ever seen. And, of course, it should immediately be put in a place of honor. Put it up in a place where it can be seen by all family members and visitors.

Your child's new skill maybe riding his bobby car or climbing stairs by himself; it may be he can wash his hands or put on his socks without help. Awesome! Praise and endorse this behavior. You may think that seems unauthentic? Or maybe even exaggerated?

Of course you are not supposed to praise to your child if it is inept. Stay true to yourself and use words you really mean. But by all means honor your child's achievement. Are you already doing it? Great! Most people know that it is important to praise a child. But do you praise him for learning things even if they are only small steps from your perspective? Because those small steps are definitely important as well.

Many adults have difficulties to give or accept praise. They think they are giving their child sufficient attention, however, what often happens in reality is the following:

Your child is approaching you with their self-painted picture:

    a. You take a look at the picture and laugh (either at it or about it), your praise may be limited to "yes that's nice".

    b. You briefly praise it and then immediately make suggestions on

> how your child could improve his work, where he has to pay closer attention to not draw over the lines or how he could make the picture look more real.

c. You hardly look at it and while you're already turning away to do something more important you say "the picture looks nice".

With this kind of praise you diminish or destroy the pride and the joy of something that is self-created, part of the learning process. You curb the enthusiasm to learn, to try new things and to be creative. Rather than pointing out where your child has not colored within the lines, you'd be better to comment on the parts where he has. If you always point out to your child what he is not so good at, what still needs to be tidied or reworked, it will eventually lead your child to expect only negative criticism whenever he approaches you. He will not believe in himself anymore when you are around. He might even start avoiding you, because honestly, who likes to be criticized all the time?

Therefore, do not point out shortcomings or something he cannot do yet. Emphasize what works well, the progress that is evident. Praise at least as much as you criticize (or make correcting suggestions). Better yet, praise a little more. Try to reach a 1:4 balance. For each piece of critical feedback make four positive statements.

Ideas Toolkit

What did you think when you read the first part of this book? Did you feel provoked? Maybe you caught yourself thinking sentences such as: *"When I was a child, I wasn't praised all the time, or very much. I didn't get pampered. I too had to work hard for everything."*

But can you also remember how disappointed or desperate you may have been by this? Do you realize how difficult it may be for you to give praise today? Even if you actually share your child's joy, you may feel worn out from your day and all you want is some peace and quiet. Talking is too much effort. Or could it be only a lack of experience that keeps you from expressing praise?

Try it! I am sure you will enjoy giving praise. People, who have not been praised themselves, often have also not learned to appreciate the small joys of life. They have not been shown the beautiful things in life. Affection and the attention of their parents may have been limited to filling their room with toys. However, they still had to play alone.

You now have the chance to rediscover all the beautiful little things in life with your child. One of them is being praised. Soon you won't want to live without it.

---

[1] Translator's note: While the German pronoun for "child" is gender neutral ("it"), in English one has to decide whether the child in question is male or female. As this book addresses parents of boys and girls alike, the translator and the author have decided to use "he" in one chapter and "she" in the next.

2. ENHANCE AND REINFORCE DESIRED BEHAVOIR

Usually kids have a pretty good idea of what they are good at and what not; what they did right or wrong and what they are capable of.

That alone is a good enough reason to not emphasize flaws and for example, stop pointing out to your child that she still cannot tie her shoelaces by herself or that she cannot juggle numbers in the thousands; that she cannot color a picture within the outlines or does not dare to go to the bakery by herself. All this is only going to reinforce her inability to do such things and will reduce your child's self-esteem. To stress her inability is neither helpful nor does it enhance learning a new skill. On the contrary, your child will eventually come to believe that she is useless.

Keep emphasizing over and over, all the things that she can already do, what she dares to try and what she has done especially well, thus, strengthening your child's confidence. In order to endorse her even more, you can link the things she has already learned with new challenges. For instance, tell her that because she is already good at riding a scooter and inline-skating, she will probably soon master riding a bike as well.

The matter of negation

If I were to prompt you at this very moment not to think of a pink pig, what do you do? You think of a pink pig. In the following I briefly want to explain the reasons behind the fact that you cannot do anything else if you hear a negation such as the above.

- Our unconscious mind works with visualization that processes visual imagery really fast. The "pink pig" is such a visual image. Our unconscious mind takes on such an image and only afterwards a "no" gets allocated to it. That means the visualization happens first and then afterwards it has to be deleted in a further cognitive step.

- Our unconscious mind does not know negation. It cannot "not" take on a visual picture. On the contrary: It constantly creates images. The conscious mind has to add the "no" in hindsight, practically putting a ban on thinking.

So, if you tell your child to n o t forget her lunch box, she first takes on the combination of "forget" and "lunch box". If you tell her n o t to slide down the waterslide backwards, the train of thought goes roughly:

"waterslide, backwards, great idea, let's go…"

Only afterwards, much too late, is it followed by "no".

Therefore, it is much better to express any form of instruction in a positive way. Tell your child what she is supposed to do: "Take your lunch box to school!" or "Please slide down the waterslide forwards and sitting down!"

Showing appreciation

School is a tiresome topic in many families, but it should not take up too much space, neither in your day-to-day life nor here. Realize how school teaches your child her "value". Someone is good and valuable if her actions lead to good grades. If your child fails in doing so, a major devaluation takes place. That makes it even more important that you give your child the confidence that she is valuable despite bad grades at school. Maybe she is good at other things that are not so important at school: baking a cake, playing soccer, giving comfort to a friend, building a space shuttle, playing with her little sister, constructing toy roads, cuddling, sensing and naming emotions, going fishing, dressing dolls, playing video games, using a cellphone, playing with Lego, making a salad, standing up for someone else's interests, being perceptive to moods, drawing faces, dancing etc. etc. The point being, she can do things that are not measured by school grades and you accept her for what she is.

Liberate yourself from thinking school could tell you something about the value of your child. Instead, make your child feel appreciated as often as you can.

Ideas Toolkit

School plays an important role in society. School played an important role in your life also. Are you still afraid of school and of authority? Have you been traumatized or were you just not good at school?

Have you only ever had your shortcomings pointed out or the things that did not work so well? Did your parents role model this kind of thinking? Do you only focus on what does not work so well now? Have you been instilled to believe that only people who were good at school are clever?

Did you only receive affection if you did things well and correctly? Did the people in your social environment react with disinterest and turn away if something did not go well at the first attempt?

Do you want your child to have better chances on the job market than you had? Do you believe with your school-leaving qualification you will always have to work in a job you do not enjoy? Do you want your child to be better off than you one day? Do you think with this background, the only way to achieve this is to constantly point out the mistakes your child makes, so she will sit down and study hard?

If you have answered to some of these questions with a resounding "yes", then you already know why it is so hard to encourage your child instead of constantly drawing her deficiencies to attention. Now ask yourself: When is learning easier for you? When someone tells you how bad you are, or if someone brings all the things to your attention that you are already good at and what you have already achieved?

3. LEAD NOT ARGUE

Think of the following situation: You want to go shopping and your child to accompany you. You are in a hurry and want to go straight away. If you ask your child if he wants to come shopping with you, you are going to risk a negation. After all, you have given your child the choice. What now? You have to either convince your child somehow or use the sledgehammer approach.

If you want things to happen in a particular way (to which there are no alternatives) and expect your child to behave accordingly, then don't ask in the first place! State clearly what you expect or wish to happen.

Let's illustrate this with another example: Your child is supposed brush his teeth before going to bed. If you already know the reply when you ask "Do you want to go bed?", then you have lost.

The same applies for "Do you want to brush your teeth?" There is no other option to brushing his teeth. State clearly what your child needs to do, instead of suggesting he has a choice.

Situations like the above occur regularly in everyday life. They harbor unnecessary seeds of conflict. If your child is supposed to get dressed quickly, then it would be best to tell him at the same time what exactly to put on, instead of giving him the choice between the jeans from the day before or the new pants from Aunty Jane. If it takes forever to decide, things will go badly for you and your time schedule.

If you as parents want something, state clearly what it is:

"Come on, get dressed! We have to go shopping!"

"First we are going to brush your teeth and then off to bed!"

"We are late, put on your jeans and then let's go!"

Otherwise you are going to transfer all power and decision-making competence to your child, burdening him with the responsibility. Especially younger children need clear statements and instructions from their parents. It will take a few years until they have learned to decide what is right and appropriate. However, if the child feels overwhelmed, he cannot make decisions and might become fretful (on top of everything else) or flinch from the task altogether. He might make a decision contrary to your wishes. At which point you may have to confront and argue with your child, aggressively defending your interests against your child's. Furthermore you are implying your child had a choice that in reality never existed.

Ideas Toolkit

When you were a child did you always have to do what your parents, grandparents or your teachers wanted? Did it confuse you when you were given a choice that was then not respected? Did you feel constrained and restricted? Unfree? But out of fear of punishment would you not dare to rebel against this injustice? Did you feel you were powerless or treated unfairly?

You probably decided that you were going to treat your children differently. That is commendable. You thought your child should have it better, grow up more freely. However, make sure that you do not expect too much of him and make him feel insecure. Do not mislead him into believing he has a choice when in reality alternatives are out of the question. All of us sometimes need a little guidance. Clear instructions are more helpful than arguments.

4. ADMITTING MISTAKES

You will find yourself in situations where you have to tell your child where she can improve, or when you think she has done something wrong. You should tell her promptly and avoid raising the subject later.

While you are at it, why not tell your child about your own imperfections, your own weaknesses or mistakes. Why not laugh together about these. This is a way to avoid creating an even bigger power imbalance between you and your child. A power imbalance exists without a doubt, simply because from your child's perspective you possess more knowledge and can do so incredibly much more than she can.

Do not increase this power gap by presenting yourself as an infallible all-rounder. It relieves your child to hear that you also do things wrong at times, do not know everything or have made mistakes in the past. That takes the pressure off her to be perfect and brings you both closer.

Time and again I meet teenagers or young adults whose biggest desire is to hear that their parents may have once messed up 'something big time', were wrong or in certain situations simply insecure. Do not be afraid to address these things. One day you child will find out anyway that you do not know or cannot do everything.

Ideas Toolkit

Parents need to be able to withstand contradictions. One of them is: wanting to be a perfect role model and pass on as much knowledge, skills and values as possible, while on the other hand, to climb down from that position and admit their own mistakes.

Hold on a moment: climb down? Feeling small, even humiliated? That is not what is meant here. But this is what parents seem to feel, who are insecure (and often not only in the relationship with their child). They enjoy being the big ones, being able to decide everything. They try to hide mistakes from their child, because they think she is not able to understand them yet. They do not want to risk to be pushed off their pedestal. They do not want their child to question their role as parents.

Do not misuse especially younger children as confidantes or substitute partners. Relieve them though, from the feeling of shame or worthlessness by admitting that everyone makes mistakes at times. You included.

5. ADMITTING KNOWLEDGE GAPS

Consider the following situation: You and your child are playing a quiz or you are helping him with his homework. He asks you something – and as you have already found out, kids sometimes ask a lot of questions, uncomfortable questions. They seem to have a seventh sense for those things you do not know. How do you react? Do you feel the need to be able to answer every question without hesitation?

Why do you not admit every now and then that there are some things you know little or nothing about? That there are certain subjects you have no idea about? If you do, you take the pressure off yourself and enable your child to develop the feeling that in some areas he can do something better or knows more. This strengthens your child's self-confidence and motivates him to look around inquisitively and eager to learn. If you give him the feeling that you already constantly know everything (better), you discourage him. Whenever possible, get your child to explain his homework to you, instead of playing the co-teacher. Secretly enjoy when you child proudly explains some facts to you. Could you endure the role reversal?

Ideas Toolkit

If you find it difficult to endure, try to consciously feel what it is like having to admit a knowledge gap. Have you always felt like a "loser", a misfit, someone who has to hide how stupid she/he feels? Often it is exactly our own inner insecurity that leads us to pretend on the outside we are especially confident and clever. Finally, in the relationship with your child, you feel you're in a position where you can play the role of the omniscient, supreme parent. If your child adores you, you feel exalted. You get to be his idol and your self-esteem is flattered.

Who would sacrifice such an appreciation that can be experienced every day, for a display of ignorance? But if you try to elevate yourself in this way, you allocate a role to your child that you are trying to rid yourself of. Step out of these constricting roles, together with your child. No one knows nor can do everything. "I know that I know nothing" – this is how Plato cited his teacher Socrates. Neither of the two philosophers can be regarded as stupid or ignorant.

6. REACHING THE LIMIT

Whether you have one child or several, if you are working or not – there will come a day that you feel you have reached the breaking point. Maybe you have had another bad night's sleep; maybe you are ill or simply exhausted. Your child infuriates you with her behavior. Those feelings are human. We all have those days when where we are at our limits.

It is important to notice the warning signs. Instead of denying that you are possibly behaving unfairly, you should recognize when you have overstepped a line or reacted aggressively and the whole situation is in danger of getting out of hand. Is your child not doing what she is supposed to do, despite yelling and threats? Are you forever fighting the same battles and simply at your limit? Then, first of all, please take a step back, because you will hardly come to a reasonable and acceptable solution in this situation.

One of the reasons for this is based on our brain activities. In conflict situations that slowly but increasingly escalate, the part of our brain that is responsible for the signals "fight or flight" will gain the upper hand. That means your thinking, your thought processes deviate from your usual cognitive abilities. Depending on the intensity of the argument, your cognitive abilities can be diminished by up to 30 per cent – that applies to both parties involved. Subsequently your ability to judge and assess the situation appropriately is greatly reduced. You will hardly reach your child by appealing to her common sense in such a moment.

Ideas Toolkit

You are not a bad person when you reach a point at which all you want to do is yell or fear you will lose your temper and hit your child. However, it is important that you recognize those situations early and change course. Leave the room; create a physical distance that can help you reach an emotional distance. Let time pass before you take up the confrontation again – give it a whole day if you have to.

If the matter that provoked the conflict is still current, start a new attempt to solve the problem, but take a different approach this time. Explain your anger and try something entirely different. Tackling the problem in the same way as before is probably useless. It has not worked the first (or several) time(s) round. Try something new.

7. EXPLAIN YOUR OWN WRONGDOINGS PROMPTLY

Arguing has to be learned – and grown-ups make mistakes too. If you have treated your child unfairly or unreasonably, it would be good to apologize directly and explain your wrongdoings. The younger the child, the more quickly this should happen.

Maybe you were in a hurry and wanted to quickly enforce something. Did you want your child to do a particular thing? Did your child want to do something completely different? Were there tears, yelling or squabbling? Did you feel guilty after things had calmed down and you realized that you reacted excessively or unjustly?

Please go to your child, explain your behavior and apologize. Children are happily willing to forgive, if they understand what happened. Additionally, you enable your child to match what his feelings with your explanations. If your child then realizes that he can trust his own feelings, he will feel more confident in similar situations and develop a stronger sense of justice. By contrast, if you deny having done anything wrong, you will make your child insecure in this regard.

We all make mistakes. If you apologize for your mistakes, you also teach your child that it is not so bad to do something wrong. One can reflect on them, get to new insights and apologize for the mistakes that were made. Your child learns to forgive other people's mistakes. It clears the air and relieves tension. It paves the way for a conciliatory new beginning.

If possible do not let many days or weeks go by before you apologize. That way it is easier for your child to relate to what has been said and to forgive. If you realize months or years later that a former reaction or decision had been wrong, you can assume that your child has had the same thought. He might bear a grudge against you or is irritated or angry because he has had to deal with the consequences of this decision for all this time. Take a quiet hour to apologize. That will give both of you the opportunity to approach each other and reconcile. Children and teenagers already know that it is only human to make mistakes. What they do not like is that grown-ups at times pretend a mistake never happened.

Ideas Toolkit

Do you generally find it hard to admit a mistake or apologize to your child? Some adults seem to think that they will end up in a less favorable position. Are you one of those people who strive to be perfect in everything you do? Does your urge for perfection legitimate you to dismiss other people's rights? Or do you feel the compulsion to never make any mistakes? Or on the contrary, do you feel uncertain about your part as a role model or parent? Are you worried about losing your authority if you admit a mistake? Do you feel small and insignificant, when you have to apologize? Someone who knows about his/her own strengths is not shaken by admitting to having done something wrong and taking responsibility for it. If you have difficulties admitting a mistake, it might be good to think about how you can strengthen your own confidence without having to hide behind a mask of perfection.

8. SETTING AN EXAMPLE

It is quite simple, really: If you want your child to behave a certain way, you have to set an example. However, many parents do exactly the opposite of what they want their children to do. It is one thing, if you drink a glass of wine on the weekend when your children are in bed, and (hopefully!) prohibit your children from drinking alcohol. It is completely different, however, if you want your children to not eat sweets, but regularly eat sugary things in front of your children. Do you want your child to stop at a red light and wait for green? Then do the same. The same rule applies to other situations.

If you want your child to go and play outside instead of spending too much time in front of the computer, then pull yourself together and set an example. If you do not want your child constantly demanding to watch TV, ask yourself how often she sees you sitting in front of the TV.

Another recurring source of conflict is at dining table. You probably would like your child to sit still and enjoy her food. Not happening? Could it be that you are a source of unrest? That you keep standing up to get something? Observe yourself. Do you suddenly get up when you are full or answer the phone during dinner time? Do you even read the newspaper at the table or watch TV? In my practice, I have met parents who seriously wonder why their children fidget so much at the dinner table while they themselves check their emails or write text messages during family meals.

Children learn from adults by imitating their behavior. For your child it is not easily comprehensible and it demands a lot of inner discipline to behave entirely different from the adults around her. If your child is not allowed to copy what she observes you doing day to day, you deprive her from the chance to learn in a manner typical for children. In some instances, such as the glass of wine or the evening crime show on TV, exceptions can be explained. But how do you want to convey to your child that she is supposed to eat in a civilized manner if you munch and slurp or spill your food?

Ideas Toolkit

You might have felt a little uneasy reading the last part. After all, it is you who makes sure dinner is on the table on time, who serves it and who goes to great lengths that everything is perfect. If a glass is missing or a fork, is it always you who gets up to get it? How about you try to involve the rest of the family as well? Could you delegate tasks instead?

What does your own reward system look like? If you squeeze in a little favor for a friend, (in between rushing around between your job, your housework, your kids and your partner) do you need a piece of chocolate for quick energy, or the whole bar? How do you rest in the evenings? How do you relax? How do you cope with boredom? Do you blob out in front of the TV? Do you simply want to consume, because you are too exhausted to engage in any meaningful activity?

If so, it is time to try to declutter your daily routine, instead of frantically cramming in as much as possible. If you notice that you exhibit behaviors that you criticize in your children, try to find the reasons why and try to find a way to ease the burden. It does not hurt to delegate jobs, to not be perfect at everything. It does not always have to be a three-course meal. It is much more important that you get to enjoy your family meals together. Soon you will notice that your child will sit and eat much calmer, if you try to be more calm yourself, innerly as well as externally.

9. ESTABLISH CLEAR RULES

„Rules are made to be broken", goes the proverb. For children however, rules are signposts providing reliability and security. Alongside rules, consistent and unambiguous behavior on the part of the parents is crucial.

Establishing rules can be useful every time you feel that conflicts or undesired behavior are repeating themselves, and, if you think there is a chance that those situations can be improved by adhering to rules. The following example might illustrate this: Until now you have helped your child get dressed in the mornings. Now you feel that your child is capable of dressing himself. But he refuses and demands you to help him. You, however, would like a little more time to yourself in the bathroom in the mornings and you insist that he becomes more independent. So, each and every morning there is a battle, but because you are responsible that your child gets to kindergarten or school on time, you give in and end up helping him to get dressed. Consequently, you eventually end up doing this grudgingly leading to tears and squabbling.

Another example: Your child comes home from school and there is homework to be done. After lunch, he first wants to play, which you find totally understandable. However, you also know that he is not going finish his homework if he plays first – or that there will be a battle when you have to tear him away from playing.

In situations such as the above it has proven useful to establish clear rules that all parties play by. First of all, it is important that you discuss these rules with your partner – unless you are a single parent. Consider whether both of you are really going to manage to introduce the rule and actually stick to it, because you will only be successful if you pull together as a team.

In order to understand why it is so important to adhere rigidly to the rules, try to picture your child's life as a path between two boundaries. If those boundaries are set too tight, the path will be too narrow for your child, who, as a result, has to over-adapt to such overly strict parenting. If the boundaries are set too far apart or if there are there none at all, then the child lacks orientation: Where is he supposed to go? The child suffers from the absence of boundaries because on his path he is looking for some form of guidance to travel by, something to give him security. If he cannot find anything he will keep looking and act accordingly. In such a situation of feeling insecure and overwhelmed, he may develop behavior that you are not going to like. He might be aggressive towards other children or adults, destroy things, establish his own "rules" or develop rituals that might appear senseless, but might provide him with a feeling of security. If you leave your child to his own devices, he will increasingly find it difficult to accept boundaries or rules. From this sense of insecurity he will provoke others and constantly challenge you. Once you have reached this stage, it will be difficult to introduce rules. If you decide to do so, it is even more important to make sure that you consistently stick to them in your daily life.

Imagine you set up a rule, but do not stick to it. What is going to happen? Although you have outlined the boundaries on the map, your child notices that if he tries to hold on to them and use them as orientation, these boundaries yield or break under the slightest pressure. If he repeatedly experiences this, he will not take these or other rules seriously anymore.

Most parents are probably aware that they neither want to impose too many restrictions nor to dissolve all boundaries around their child. If you live in a relationship then it is paramount that you only establish rules that you both agree on. If you need to discuss controversial points, please do not do this in front of your children. Also do not belittle your partner's opinion, for instance, by rolling your eyes or groaning. For your children this would mean that it is okay to sometimes stick to the boundaries and sometimes not. If one cannot hold on to them, then why do they exist?

Ideas Toolkit

Many parents confuse clear, unambiguous behavior with harshness and aggression. Especially parents who experienced corporal punishment as a child or were constantly yelled at by their own parents, who suffered under aggressive and authoritarian parents, often do not know how to assert themselves without following their own parents' example. Or they just helplessly allow things to continue as they are – shying away from setting limits. They may eventually succumb to their own parents' negative parenting role model.

If you feel stuck between a rock and a hard place, try to remind yourself that consistent parenting is not a punishment. Children with alcoholic parents report that they have suffered under the unpredictable behavior of living with addicts. Depending on their parents' mood, they were either lifted to the heavens with praise or other times, blamed scolded for nothing. Sometimes the rules applied, sometimes they did not. It causes the same insecurity as the "boundless" child. The same happens, if you use your children as leverage in disagreements between you and your partner i.e. if you allow your child to do something your partner has forbidden, in order to bias your child towards you. Not only do you harm your relationship, you also harm your child.

IF YOU EAT TWO MORE BROCCOLI FLORETS AND THREE SPOONFULS OF RICE AND DRINK AT LEAST FOUR SEVENTHS OF YOUR TEA, THEN YOU MAY WATCH TV FOR 14 MINUTES.
WE AGREED ON FIVE SEVENTHS! I DON'T UNDERSTAND WHY YOU KEEP STABBING ME IN THE BACK!

10. INVOLVING CHILDREN IN TASKS

To eat with a spoon, to dress or undress yourself, to climb stairs, to butter your sandwich, to unlock a door with a key, to turn a page, to read, to switch on a light, to slice a cucumber, to make a phone call, to paint a picture, to tie your shoelaces...

Your child's universe is full of tasks he has to learn and perform every day. Initially, not everything will go smoothly and he will be a little clumsy when learning a new skill. Yet, try not to do everything for him. Dedicate your time and patience to your child. Praise him for every little progress and every task he has managed. Once he learns to do something by himself, something he needed your help with before, then let him do it by himself from now on.

Consider though, is it too dangerous? Maybe your child wants to do something by which he could get hurt? No one is going to expect you to let him try to see how far he can lean over the balcony railing before falling down. However, if it concerns less perilous things – slicing a cucumber or pouring himself a glass of water, walking down the stairs, peeling a potato, swinging higher, riding a balance bike or climbing a climbing-wall – then you should allow him to do so. Hold yourself back but stay close to intervene quickly if needed.

If you are taking things out of your child's hands too quickly (either because you are impatient or because you do not trust in his abilities), he will begin to question his own abilities and become less venturous. He will regard supposedly harmless situations and activities as difficult. Eventually, you will ask yourself why your child is so dependent and diffident.

I do not want to encourage you to be careless, reckless or negligent. That is something entirely different. Be attentive and allow your child to try by himself and to enjoy learning new skills.

Ideas Toolkit

There are many reasons why parents over-protect their children and try to shield them from danger or painful experiences. Some of them are worried they are making a mistake when they do not supervise their child at all times. They are worried something bad might happen and that in hindsight they might be accused of being inattentive. These people are often particularly dependent on other peoples' opinions in other areas and they try to please everyone or certain people, such as their parents or parents-in-law. They cannot bear being criticized; they always have to deliver 110 per cent. In short, they fear taking a "risk" that other people do not regard as risk.

A second group that tends to strongly protect their own children consists of people who have had no or little protection as children themselves. They might have been bullied by other children or authorities at kindergarten or school and had no one to whom they could turn to for help. If you belong to one of these categories (or for other reasons have a tendency to not have much confidence in your child, or find it hard to let go) try observing other parents. How do they handle situations?

How big is the danger really? What would be worse for your child: to fall off the swing or to have never experienced how wonderful it is to swing up high?

11. YOU WANT YOUR CHILD TO BE HAPPY ALL THE TIME?

Do you like to pamper your child? Are you shielding her from all difficulties? Do you find it hard to see her suffering? Do you want her not to be burdened with sickness or do you avoid anything risky where she could hurt herself?

Do you smother-love your child until an age where she is about to leave school? Do you battle with teachers at kindergarten or at school? Do you want your child to be the special focus of attention?

If this is the case your child has a problem and I'm sorry, unfortunately it's you!

No one in this world would claim that they want their child to be unhappy, but how do we support our children to experience as many happy moments as possible? Surely not by saving them from all potential challenges or from situations in which they could experience fear or which we regard a little dangerous.

Does your child bravely climb a chair or a tree? Does she have to visit the dentist? Is the first day of kindergarten or school drawing closer? Does she like to ride a scooter or inline skates? Do you find her being harassed by other kids on the way home from school? Does she have to deal with aggressive behavior on the soccer field? If so, support her but do not shield her from activities or experiences like the above.

Supporting means, first of all, standing back! You child needs challenges and to encounter difficulties without your assistance. This is the only way she learns to tackle those situations and to develop courage. If in doubt, ask yourself: will your child rise to the challenge or will she break down under the burden? It is better to wait a little bit longer and stay alert but in the background. Your child is capable of more than you think!

Of course, your child is not supposed to break down under the tasks she has to master. Do not demand too much of her and ensure that the challenges she encounters are age appropriate. She should be allowed to confront challenges. Only by learning to overcome difficult tasks and situations, will she become proficient at accepting challenges, handling them, and searching for solutions. She discovers new ways around problems and learns what it feels like to have found a solution by herself. This experience is going to boost her, so that she will be able to successfully handle new challenges – which certainly will arise one day. This way your child can feed on a wealth of experience that will help her to stand up for herself in uncertain or difficult situations. If you take away your child's opportunity to learn by making her own experience, you take away her chance to develop her own strategies and to prove herself confident and independent when encountering problems. By the way, this is still true even if your child has to find out that unfortunately, there might not be a solution to every problem.

Ideas Toolkit

Did you ever experience neglect in your childhood or had to struggle through everything on your own, because your parents did not care for you or just did not have time for you? Do you want to compensate the suffering that you experienced by sheltering your child from similar experiences?

Do you regard your child as a helpless little creature that cannot handle difficulties or withstand any pain?

If you as a child had to endure highly humiliating, painful or fearful situations, then it merits you if this resulted in you being sympathetic towards your child rather than being overly strict. If no one attended to your childhood worries and needs, it is understandable that you want to act differently with your own children.

Yet, ask yourself: do you want your child to grow up to be a confident, independent person? Or to be fearful, assimilated and meek?

You might have had to cope with burdens in your childhood that were not age appropriate. However, the simple fact that you worry about these things and try to protect and care for your child means that your child will grow up under different circumstances to yours. In you, she has a person who is approachable, supportive and nurturing. So instead of trying to shield her from any unpleasant situations, support her to cope with them.

If you were not exposed to any particular stress during your childhood, consider your fear of criticism that could mislead you to overprotect your child. Are you worried that someone will hold your mistakes against you or that you might be accused of being negligent? If so, what will you do when your child grows older and escapes your supervision? You will not be able to control your child forever. You can only help her prepare to manage difficult situations.

12. ALLOWING UNPLEASANT EMOTIONS

Your child is running, falls and grazes his knee. He cries and calls out for you. He is startled and there is a burning pain in his knee. What do you do? The usual reaction would be to go to him, look at his knee and tell him: "It's not that bad. It's going to be okay. Stop crying!" Why do you do that? Why is your child not allowed to cry – because you cannot endure his pain?

If your child is sad, angry, and anxious or is in pain, let him feel that sensation for a moment. Just for a small moment acknowledge this feeling, confirm it. Allow your child to feel the way he does. Count to 20 to yourself if your own anguish begins to overwhelm you, but avoid denying your child his feelings by trying to make everything okay again. Dress the wound, hold your child and comfort him. Once he has calmed down, there will still be plenty of time for giving advice.

The same applies to situations where your child has to learn to deal with frustrating experiences.

An example:

Your child builds an intricate sand castle at the beach. A ball comes flying and lands directly on the sand castle. Everything is destroyed. Your child bursts into tears. The usual reaction again is to go to your child, hug him and say something like: "It's okay. It's only sand. You can rebuild it".

By displaying this kind of behavior you want to help your child to overcome his grief. But burying feelings is not the same as 'staying with them' and eventually to process them. Therefore, do not act according to the maxim: the main thing is that the child does not suffer and everything runs smoothly again! If you do that, you will convey the message that these emotions are undesired. You are teaching him that he will not be accepted because of his emotions. Instead acknowledge what happened, your child's place is in all of it and how he feels. Then help him deal with it.

Ideas Toolkit

Often it is much harder to bear the woes of people we love than our own. In particular, when it comes to children we are often tempted to rush in and make everything alright again. Additionally, it might be uncomfortable if your child cries and screams in public and cannot be calmed down easily. Many people feel embarrassed if they attract attention. They feel inadequate if they fail to comfort their child quickly. They somehow feel guilty, either that their child is unhappy in the first place or that they are unable to ease this grief quickly.

To allow your child to stay with his feelings means to take him seriously. Instead of trying to blow the pain away or brushing his emotions aside, take him in your arms, hold him for a moment and let him cry and scream. Soothe him and maybe rock him gently (depending on his age). Wait a little while; confirm his feeling ("That really hurts") and just hold him. Afterwards ask questions: "Did you trip over that silly rock? Did you get a fright? Gently try to move that leg; can you do that again? Yes? Okay, let's go…".

The destroyed sand castle could also be a trigger for a situation such as the above. The same applies here: For a moment just be there and be compassionate towards him instead of immediately trying to make everything okay again. Confirm the validity of the feeling ("What a shame — such a great sand castle!") and hold your child. Then you can begin to offer alternatives: "Do you want to rebuild it or do you want to do something else instead?" Or "Shall we rebuild it together? Come on, I will help you!"

You notice the differences in the ways to respond are only minimal, yet crucial. Allow your child to feel pain, disappointment, anger or sadness. At the same time he learns that you want to support and comfort him. Only afterwards can you slowly change the situation with suggestions or taking action or new ideas. Asking questions is a good starting point for this.

13. NO COMPARISONS WITH OTHER KIDS!

Do you have two or more children, and did your first child learn faster, more skillful and in general better than the other ones? Or do you have the feeling that your neighbor's child of the same-age child can do more things than yours?

Maybe yes. But even if this might be the case: Please do <u>not</u> point it out to your child – because you would not be doing her a favor. All you achieve is to put more pressure on her. Being under pressure and tension blocks the ability to learn. Your child will feel depreciated and incompetent. Unable to change her situation, she will feel powerless against the "superior qualities" of the other child. So she will begin to feel dumb and worthless. Her self-esteem disappears.

Of course, you had more time and patience with your first born. Now, you have to divide your time and energy between two or more children. It is normal to wish that the younger ones could help as much and were as independent as the eldest.

Is your youngest behind at school? Or does she just take a little bit longer or has a different learning style? Does she respond to different approaches? Is the role of the child who does especially well at school, already occupied in your family? Does she even have a chance to be praised for her comparatively "smaller" successes?

In any case, you should refrain from continuously pointing out inadequacies that only became apparent by comparison with other children. Stay patient and try to convey educational content in a different way. Simply wait. Trust that this child will also learn eventually, in her own time. Does she exhibit specific strengths at other things? Does she have particular interests? Then encourage and praise these features.

Ideas Toolkit

You worry about the future of your child. You want her to make something of herself. You want her to be better off one day. You have tried so many approaches, starting with putting her under mild pressure to coaxing her; you would even like to increase the pressure, so she will be faster, more active and better.

Unfortunately, putting on pressure does the opposite of what you want: Your child will be stressed even more, and stress hormones reduce our brain's performance. As a result, we are even less successful than before. This leads to more stress – trapping us in a vicious cycle.

You might notice that with your second, third, fourth child, you lack energy to do all the things that you took in your stride with your first. Maybe it would be better for this child to change schools? Would it help, if you talked to her teachers or found other forms of learning? Do you even dare to argue with your child's teachers? Many parents avoid conflicts with school and instead demand that their children should "perform" better. However, in the end it is important to understand: No comparison is going help your child to improve. Take her as she is. Grant her individual learning speed, her talents, weaknesses, and abilities to prove herself in life – with or without top grades.

BRILLIANT!
ER - BOTH OF YOU.

14. BOREDOM

Many children cannot appreciate spare time anymore and become easily bored. They are used to going to kindergarten, being occupied and entertained by gymnastic classes, soccer, horse riding, early language classes, music lessons, as well as school. The times when there is no program to follow, they do not know what to do with themselves. Watching TV, playing video games or spending time in front of the computer offer distraction, but they do not change the underlying problem: they have not learned to play creatively and by themselves. The moment you take the remote control out of their hands, they will start whining. They do not do this out of spite, but they simply cannot occupy themselves. The child is unable to keep himself busy, because most of his short life he has been directed by others.

And how about you? How quickly do you give in?

Try to endure your child's boredom! After having overcome this initial phase, in which your child realizes that you are not going to entertain him, he will begin to look for alternatives. And usually he will find something. If this experience is repeated, he will return to this behavior, thus, learning to occupy himself independently and creatively.

So, instead of offering a solution, encourage your child to find (or invent) an activity by himself. For instance, ask him what he would like to do right now. Perhaps he would like to build something or paint a picture? Questions like these stimulate the creative search process.

Do not expect his approval straight away. In many cases initially the situation seems hopeless and you and you child feel at a loss. Nevertheless, stay firm and wait. Little by little ideas will pop up and every time the process is repeated, it will work more smoothly. State clearly that you will not always be available for playing. Show him that you are busy doing other important things – such as household chores – and that you do not have time at the moment. Re-examine on occasion if it would be better for your child to have more spare time, instead of being entertained day after day.

Ideas Toolkit

Children need inspiration, and there are no objections if your child plays soccer or the piano. However, occasional boredom is the engine for creativity. Make sure that your child is familiar with the concept of spare time, which he has to structure and fill in by himself. Provide him with material that he can use to create, build, or make something instead of showering him with expensive but nonproductive toys. Also look at toys from this perspective: Is a toy only good for a single purpose or can it be used to create something on you own?

A cardboard box, a glittering stone or a stick can all be transformed easier than a plastic castle or an electronic beeping action figure. The cardboard box could be a house or a store today, and a car tomorrow; the stone has magic powers; the stick will be a sword or a divining staff. Do not restrict your child's imagination; allow his mind to roam freely. You are going to be surprised how contently the former whingy child can spend his free time.

NOT EVEN HALF AN HOUR IN THE FRESH AIR WITHOUT A TV OR A VIDEO GAME CONSOLE AND OUR SON HAS BUILT HIMSELF A CAVE.
A REACTOR, DAD. IT'S A NUCLEAR REACTOR.

15. PLAYING WITH ADULTS

But what if your child doesn't find anything to do or does not want to build anything or draw? Then once again the following applies:

Leave your child alone with her boredom. Allow that she – from your perspective – fritters away her time. Wait before you offer to play something with her. In many cases, she will look for, try out and eventually find something to play with. The experience of having found an exciting game on her own accord will make your child more autonomous and independent. In a similar situation she will remember this positive experience and start playing by herself sooner.

Once she has found a stimulating activity, it is best that you do not interrupt her. Whether you are at home or at the playground: be present, but stay in the background! Watching from afar is sufficient. If you constantly get involved and ask what interesting games she is playing, then do not be surprised if your child interrupts her game to turn her attention to you and wants you to be her play buddy.

Use the time your child is playing by herself to relax. Read the newspaper or a book, or catch up on unfinished housework. Permit yourself to be redundant right this moment.

Ideas Toolkit

In your own childhood, were you left to your own devices too often? Did you lack play offers or inspiration? Do you want to give your child all opportunities to develop, to learn something? Do you want to encourage her talents early on, so she – in whichever respect – will be better off than you one day?

This is understandable. But meanwhile many parents overshoot the mark. If you heap toys or play offers onto your child, she will be crushed by the weight of options. Overabundance often leads to disinterest.

If all you want is to be a good father or mother and you do not want to risk being accused of not having looked after your child properly, then show your child that y o u are also capable of occupying yourself; encourage her to try it out too.

16. ATTENTION NOT AMBITION

Your child has participated in an early learning program and you have taken advantage of the neurological critical period of language acquisition for your child to learn Mandarin. You have chosen this particular kindergarten because it offered the opportunity to participate in a weekly physics tutoring class. The teaching in your child's primary school is bilingual. Your child is supposed to listen to Mozart and Bach Sonatas, not because you regard it as a special treat, but because you want to take advantage of the important imprinting phase for music at this stage of her life. Of course, she takes violin lessons. At an early age, your child found a chemistry and physics experimental kit under the Christmas tree. You deliberately chose a school that has a reputation for only taking the best and that has very high expectations. From your perspective you have ideally done everything to promote your child's intelligence, thus paving her path to a great career.

Your child takes everything in her stride, right? Or do you at times get the impression she might be a little disinterested or tired of school? Does she bite her fingernails? Does she grind her teeth at night? At ten years of age, does she still wet her bed? Does she sleep badly? Has she developed anxieties or does she have difficulties finding friends her own age, because she prefers the company of adults? Is she known as the outsider? Does she start the day cheerfully or does she regularly have headaches or stomach aches? Especially on schooldays?

If your child can explain a complicated physics problem in detail to you, be happy for her – provided you can feel her enthusiasm. However, if your pride about your kid's intelligence becomes so strong that you have to show off how clever she is, then you should urgently question your motives. If your child meets YOUR high aspirations, ask yourself if she has enough space to develop her own ambitions. What about other competencies? Does she have contact with children the same age? Does she exhibit joy in the things she does? Or are all her endeavors aimed at the future?

Loving parents want the best for their children. The temptation to open up potential opportunities by excessive early education at pre-school age has never been as big as it is today. Even a parent, who does not generally agree with this, might feel somewhat uneasy that the neighbor's child is already so advanced in many respects. Playing the violin, conducting experiments, being able to explain the movement of the planets. Being able to read and write before she starts school. Doubts will start to seize hold of you; maybe your own attitude that children need unstructured time is outdated and your child will not be able to keep up with the others. Or you might be confronted with derogative remarks when your grubby offspring returns home from the playground while the neighboring kids are engaged in 'meaningful occupations'. If we do not engage our children in these supposedly meaningful occupations, do we deprive them of vital abilities they need to be successful in life?

Intelligent behavior means selecting not accumulating

Intelligent behavior is the ability to make decisions. Yet, when it comes to early childhood education the opposite seems to be true: The belief prevails, the more we fill the database of our child with information, the wealthier she will become in life. The -oh so commendable- intelligence is often equated with a successful accumulation of school knowledge. And school, as we all know, just happens to be not very interesting all the time. You slog along without knowing whether all this toil is worth the while. The longer you suffer through school, the more intelligent you will get, won't you? Or could it be that the accumulation of knowledge might not be related to intelligence after all?

And is there a plan B, in case all extra schooling is to no avail, and your child burns herself out on her ascent to the sun, instead of climbing up to the stars? Who has failed then? You? School? Your child? What value does she have then, as a person?

I do not want to demonize all early education. If your child loves playing the violin then encourage and support her talent. If she prefers reading books instead of competing at sports, then let her read. The difference in these examples is that the initial spark originates from your child. But if your child, in your eyes, is only worthy long as she fulfills the expectations of school and society, or she is equally talented in music, natural science and languages, then you really should question your own motivation about wanting the 'best' for your child.

Ideas Toolkit

Do you feel your education was supported sufficiently by your own parents? Were you just put on the side line? Did your parents want you to finish school as quickly as possible, so you could earn money and start a family? Would you have liked to have had the chance to be more successful in life and do you want to make up to your child what your parents have failed to give to you?

And how about your self-esteem? Do you think only those who have received higher education or who have distinguished themselves through special achievements are worthy members of society? Do you believe that people with a high IQ automatically have a high self-esteem? Do you feel dumb and inferior because you did not have the same educational chances as your child? Do you want to increase your own worth by proving to the world what you could have been by using your child as a surrogate? Along the lines of: "Look, what an intelligent child I have. This is my achievement! I have done everything right, so I have got to be clever. The others have to finally acknowledge this as well." Do you feel more confident? Does some of her brilliance make you shine brighter?

You can find out quite easily, whether in reality it is all about wanting the best for your child or whether subconsciously you are compensating for your own sense of inferiority. Provided you have the courage to be honest with yourself. Pay attention to what happens when your child reports a failure. Do you feel guilty? Is this "disgrace" your own disgrace? Are you personally affected by this failure? Does it reflect badly on you? Of course, we empathize with our children and we feel sorry for them if something did not turn out the way they had intended. However, if in those moments you regard this as a personal failure, then could it be that your child is carrying the heavy responsibility on her shoulders of making your life's dream come true.

The courage to be idle

I assume you work a lot (and hard) to give your children the best possible education. Or maybe you scrimp and save all your money to provide your child with music lessons and language classes. How much time do you have left for stimulating, entertaining, joyful hours with your children? And how much time do you allow your child to explore the world on her own, to reinvent the wheel?

How much leisure time does she have to develop her existing talents, instead of following prefabricated concepts for a successful life?

Playing with dolls or wooden blocks, digging in the sandpit, splashing in water, making a proper din with cooking pots, enjoying snuggly reading time, playing car races, looking at picture books, emptying out draws, painting, building things, playing sports and meeting other children. Playing theater, turning Lego blocks into little works of art, dressing the hair of cuddly toys, frolicking around the house, laughing, screaming, climbing and curiously exploring her environment. Visiting the puppet show, watching builders or refuse collectors, petting or discovering animals on the road and at the zoo. The life of a child is full of exciting surprises, even without early childhood education. Give your child the opportunity to explore her environment. Tell her something that stimulates her interests or take the time for little trips: a visit to the farm, sowing flowers, picking blackberries, exploring playgrounds. Call her attention to interesting things, but leave it up to her if she wants to dismantle her toys, look into the insides of her alarm clock or observe the stars at night.

If really you want to promote your child purposefully, find o n e challenging field or activity she is interested in. Allow her to ask her own questions and to develop her own creativity. You know from you own experience that you learn the easiest if you approach things with enthusiasm and curiosity. It does not make sense and it is a waste of time, wanting to fill your child with knowledge for answering questions that she has never asked. The best way to impart knowledge to someone is when that person displays noticeable interest in the subject. Then the brain will link information forming new ways of thinking. This creates real prior knowledge establishes and new information can build on this – real interest that will lead to further questions and initiative.

However, refrain from trying to offer 'superior' early education. Do not smother every budding interest with answers, courses, materials. Instead ask yourself, what is really important to you? Do you want your child to be clever and successful all the time or do you want her to enjoy things and activities without always having to learn something? Certainly, one thing does not exclude the other. But one day your child may have developed a completely different understanding of a successful life than you. Do not force her into your narrow frame of mind. Instead of frantically investing all your money in your child's early development, treat yourself to music lessons, a language course or catch up on things you have missed out on. Who knows, maybe it will help you to increase your confidence and you will be more relaxed when it comes to education and intelligence.

Offering learning opportunities and supporting your child of course influence the development of her intelligence. Through parents and other influencing factors such as kindergarten, friends, grandparents and school, she can learn a lot, but also allow your child to discover the world. Accompany her serenely and with patience. It is completely sufficient to just spend time with her. Time, in which you devote your attention and joy to her and offer her age-appropriate play opportunities.

Development also means personal development

When you have to choose a (secondary) school, try to rid yourself of the desire to make your choice solely on the school's promotion of performance and intelligence. The only yardstick should be your child – and her interests and talents. Therefore a school that emphasizes your child's personal development, enjoyment, self-esteem and life experience, can be much more suitable than a school that is modelled on old traditional methods and aims.

You might want to re-read the second chapter, "Enhance and Reinforce Desired Behavior", of this book, especially the part about "Showing appreciation".

The chapter "No Comparisons with Other Children!" will also hopefully be able to back your intention to support your child properly without suffocating her needs with an oversupply of toys and structured programs.

IT'S ALL ABOUT HIM DEVELOPING A SENSE FOR THE INSTRUMENT AND A GUSTO FOR THE WOOD.

CONCLUSION: WHY IS IT SO HARD?

You have read the previous pages more or less attentively. At some points you have nodded in appreciation, at others you have shaken your head in disagreement, but your overall conclusion is hopefully: These are not abstract theories or methods. This is about you, your child and your common sense. It is about you finding solutions that seem appropriate and practical to you; the most natural thing in the world, so to speak.

Most parents know what is good for their child and themselves. Why then does it seem so hard to put this knowledge into practice? Why do we not trust our ideas and intuitions? So why does your child, of all children, have to be so difficult?

I often get introduced to children who are somehow "wrong" in the eyes of their parents. I am regarded as the expert that is supposed to fix the child, so she/he will come right again. If I as a counsellor say bluntly that, in my opinion, it is not the child but the parents that need therapy; I am usually met with refusal and strong criticism – although it was the parents who asked for my opinion in the first place.

Why is that?

Parents are under pressure to do everything perfectly. Only in rare cases are they able to recognize or admit that when it comes to parenting, they are caught in their own actions and that they make mistakes, despite knowing better. At the end of each chapter under "Ideas Toolkit", I have called your attention to recurring patterns. Often I encouraged you to re-examine which ideas, beliefs, experiences, fears and hopes have shaped your style of parenting.

Did you feel considerable inner objection when reading these paragraphs? Did you dislike the wording and did you use this inner resistance as a welcome excuse to not having to deal with the content? It is this attitude of refusing to deal with your own preconditions that stand between you and your child, and you and your goals.

You might now decide to take up the next parenting guide hoping it will suggest a method or a behavior that does not include you – some advice you can follow without having to reflect on yourself. If this is the case I have failed in m y goal: the desire to illustrate that it might be more helpful to truly listen to your inner self.

We generally all know that as parents we do not live in a vacuum, but have been raised and socialized in a particular way. Still, it is an extremely difficult task to unlearn patterns even if they have harmed us as children or we regard them as inefficient or dissonant parenting methods. It may seem a little bit like having to part with our old favorite jacket. It might be a little threadbare and smelly, yet it is so comfortable to wear.

In order to part with acquired behavior you need the willingness to take an honest look at yourself and question yourself. The same is true for patterns that we have developed simply out of resistance against our own parents' parenting style. If you honestly examine those patterns, old wounds will heal; insecurities, pain and haunting memories will cease. Who would not prefer to forget all these? But is it not somewhat grotesque that we read guide after guide, visit experts and therapists in the hope to find a solution to a problem, when in reality every step takes us further away from ourselves?

For a moment close your eyes and ask yourself why it might be that you are unable to reach one or the other parenting goal, implement principles and make your child play by the rules. Does the reason really lie your child, or can the reason be found in you?

You might be disappointed now. You might have preferred advice such as the ones that (in)famous super nannies on TV give. A ten-point-plan that you cana follow step by step. But theoretical knowledge alone on how to change the outer circumstances is not enough. The initial euphoria you might feel after having received supposedly helpful advice is not going to carry you or your child to new shores. After a few days you will notice yourself reverting back to old patterns. This awareness might even cause you to feel even more ashamed or fear someone might notice your inadequacy or inability to cope with your role as a parent. Instead of being too hard on yourself, try to explore your feelings in a curious, unbiased and compassionate way. You will notice it takes a bit of courage. Keep at it. Eventually you will become more and more successful.